Sentence Mitigation Strategies

Engineer Pathways to the Highest Level of Liberty, at the Soonest Possible Time

www.WhiteCollarAdvice.com
Support@WhiteCollarAdvice.com / 818-424-2220

QR Codes

Digital Courses

The criminal justice system is complicated. Building a case for leniency, or mercy, requires a comprehensive mitigation strategy. Our digital courses can help. Access lessons, watch videos, and learn from subject-matter experts, including federal judges, wardens, probation officers, and people who've gone through every stage of the journey.

Always strive to help your defense attorney by creating resources to support arguments for leniency.

It's never too early, and never too late to begin learning how you can work toward a better outcome. Some of our free courses will help you understand:

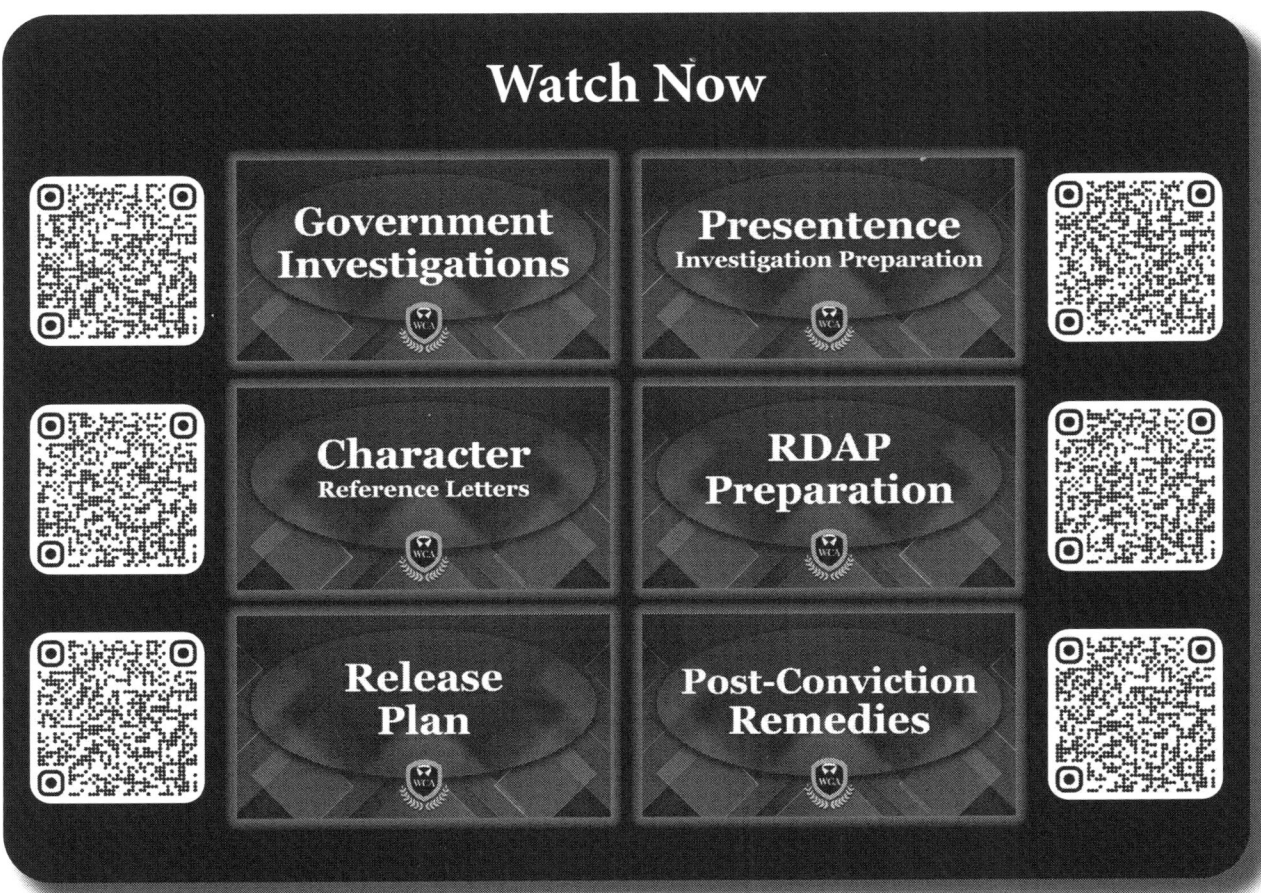

www.WhiteCollarAdvice.com / Support@WhiteCollarAdvice.com / 818-424-2220

We're not a law firm. We specialize in providing support services to defense attorneys and mitigation services to people who face criminal charges. Through this brochure, we help others understand our ecosystem, which includes:

White Collar Advice: Boutique consulting service to help people prepare mitigation strategies for various stages of the journey.

Prison Professors: Our nonprofit, which creates digital content that reaches more than 1 million people serving sentences in jails and prisons across America. The Bureau of Prisons features our course, Success after Prison, in every federal prison, as shown in its First-Step Act approved programs catalog.

Prison Professors Talent: Our nonprofit sponsors this platform, which helps people in prison memorialize their progress to reconcile with society and prepare for success upon release.

White Collar Advice Digital Courses: We create digital courses to assist people with understanding various aspects of the criminal justice system, from government investigations to post-release success.

TopWCA Legal Directory: Our legal directory is a collaboration that profiles five defense attorneys from each of the 94 different federal judicial districts. More than 1 million people visit our brands annually, and our legal directory allows defense attorneys to show their commitment to excellence.

Prison Professors Charitable Corporation: We advocate for expansion of the First Step Act and promote work-release programs, as well as more opportunities for people to earn freedom through merit and a pursuit of excellence.

Digital/Publishing Services: Our nonprofit hires formerly incarcerated individuals to create reputational management, marketing, graphic arts, and reputational management services for businesses and individuals. For an example, use the QR code below to see our digital brochure.

Follow White Collar Advice and Prison Professors on our social media channels, including YouTube, Instagram, Linked In, TicToc, Twitter, and any other channel where we can advance our commitment to improving the outcomes of America's prison system.

For more information, contact our managing partner, Justin Paperny, at JP@WhiteCollarAdvice.com / 818-424-2220.

Forward

In 1987, during the pre-guideline era of indeterminate sentencing, authorities looped me into a government investigation. Prosecutors in the Western District of Washington convened a grand jury and indicted me for operating a Continuing Criminal Enterprise.

A magistrate judge agreed with prosecutors and ordered pretrial detention. There were no allegations of weapons or violence. Yet, given the severity of my crime, officers held me in solitary confinement while awaiting trial.

United States District Court Jack Tanner presided over my trial. I made every bad decision a person could make, including,

» Pleading not guilty and proceeding through trial even though I knew I was guilty,
» Receiving profits from the ongoing crime even while I was in custody,
» Perjuring myself on the witness stand.

A jury convicted me of every count.

Following the verdict, the US Marshals returned me to the detention center. Officer Wilson passed me *The Republic* by Plato. The story of Socrates inspired me. He taught me how to think differently.

Instead of worrying about my problems, Socrates taught me to work toward reconciliation and making amends.

Officer Wilson then brought me an autobiography of Frederick Douglass.

From those two books, I began to believe that even though I had made a series of bad decisions, I could work toward leading a life of meaning, relevance, and dignity–even while serving time in prison. I set a three-pronged goal of working to:

» Learn more and earn academic credentials,
» Contributing to society in meaningful, measurable ways and
» Build a strong support network that would open opportunities to succeed upon release.

That strategy empowered me through 9,500 days in prison. While inside, I felt blessed to earn academic degrees, build a career, marry the love of my life, and build a business with my friend and partner, Justin Paperny.

All those efforts put me in a position to work toward advocacy through our nonprofit, Prison Professors, where we strive to make an impact on improving the outcomes of America's prison system.

Through this brochure, readers will learn that regardless of past decisions, it's never too early and never too late to begin sowing seeds for a better outcome. While I focus on advocacy and working to promote macro changes that include the introduction of work-release programs, home confinement, and opportunities to incentivize the pursuit of excellence, my partner Justin leads a team of dedicated professionals through our boutique consulting firm. His work supports our nonprofit efforts.

We encourage defense attorneys and people facing criminal charges to learn how they can work toward reconciliation and write the next chapter of their lives. Use the same plan that we advocate:

- » Define success as the best possible outcome,
- » Create a plan,
- » Put priorities in place,
- » Assist counsel by developing tools, tactics, and resources,
- » Become a master of self-advocacy,
- » Measure progress,
- » Adjust the plan as necessary,
- » Execute the plan daily.

This strategy will assist defense attorneys and lead participants to the highest level of liberty as soon as possible.

The one promise Justin and I make is that we will never lie to anyone, nor would we suggest anyone pursue a path that we did not take. We are transparent and public, and we encourage others to learn from our journey.

Start sowing seeds today for a higher level of liberty. It's the path to restoring confidence and working toward the next chapter of resilience.

With best wishes, I thank you for trusting in our amazing team.

Respectfully,

Michael Santos

Table of Contents

QR Codes 2

Digital Courses 3

Forward 5

Table of Contents 7

Letter from Managing Partner 8

Who We Help 10

Pre Sentence Investigation to Alec Burlakoff 14

PSR Preparation 15

RDAP 16

Digital Courses 17

Sentencing Preparation Example 18

Influencing Sentencing 19

Personal Advocacy Campaigns 20

Release Preparations 22

PrisonProfessorsTalent.com 23

Timelines 24

Be Extraordinary 26

Media Contributions 27

Academic / Professional 28

Our Team 29

Non Profit 30

Non Profit Advocacy 31

Legal Directory 33

Letter from Managing Partner

When a person learns that authorities have begun an investigation, everything in life changes. At that stage, a person must remember that it's never too early, and never too late to begin preparing for better outcomes.

But how does a person who has never been involved with the criminal justice system prepare?

Typically, the first step a person takes is to search for counsel. Sometimes, however, a person doesn't even know how to identify a competent defense attorney, or prepare in ways that will help the defense attorney best.

We excel at helping people who've been targeted for a criminal prosecution. We're not a law firm, and we don't offer legal advice. Rather, we're mitigation experts and we help people navigate crisis, regardless of what stage of the journey they're in, including:

- » Government Investigations
- » Pre-plea Contemplations
- » Presentence Investigation Preparation
- » Sentencing Preparation
- » Engineering Advocacy Campaigns
- » Coping with Sanctions
- » Developing Release Plans
- » Creating Self-Advocacy Strategies
- » Recalibrating and Rebuilding

With this brochure, we'll offer more insight into the way that we help our clients architect a plan that will help them restore confidence and begin moving toward the highest level of liberty, at the soonest possible time.

My name is Justin Paperny, and I'm the managing partner of White Collar Advice.

My partners and I created this brochure to offer more insight on how we assist people who want to learn more about how they can begin working toward the best possible outcomes. We encourage people to begin thinking about the same strategies that led to success in other areas of life.

- » Step 1: Define Success
- » Step 2: Develop a Plan
- » Step 3: Set Priorities
- » Step 4: Develop Tools, Tactics, and Resources
- » Step 5: Create Accountability Metrics
- » Step 6: Prepare to Adjust to Fluid Situations
- » Step 7: Execute the Plan

We'd like to say that we created this roadmap to success, but that wouldn't be accurate. It's the same strategy that leaders have used to overcome crises since the beginning of time. Unfortunately, the personal trauma that follows news of a government investigation, a prosecution, or a potential prison term can complicate a person's ability to navigate pathways to success.

Our team can help.

The remainder of this brochure offers more insight into how we serve our clients, including:

- » Defendants
- » Law firms
- » Media Representatives
- » All stakeholders

Start sowing seeds today for the best possible outcome.

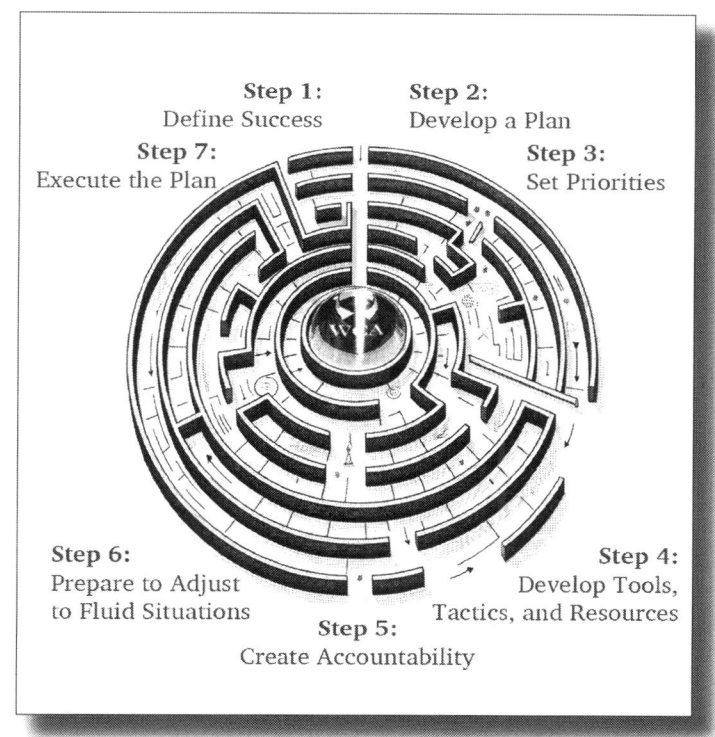

www.WhiteCollarAdvice.com / Support@WhiteCollarAdvice.com / 818-424-2220

Who We Help

Targets/Defendants

When authorities target a person for prosecution, everything changes. The charge can threaten a person's sense of peace. In that moment, the person may feel like a marionette puppet, with others pulling the strings. We assist people in developing comprehensive advocacy strategies for each stage of the journey.

Defense Attorneys

Defense attorneys are well suited to assess evidence and determine the best legal strategy. We do not interfere with that process. Rather, we help people understand how they can build tools, tactics, and resources to advance them as a candidate for leniency.

Media Representatives

Journalists need credible experts to provide commentary and nuances to different stages of the process. Our team has worked with well-known television networks, movie studios, newspapers, and magazines. We offer expert guidance that helps audiences understand various aspects of true crime and provide commentary on real-time events.

Law Firms

One of the biggest challenges of any business, including a law firm, is customer acquisition. Our legal directory can help. Through our website, TOPWCA, we profile five defense attorneys or law firms from each of the 94 different federal jurisdictions. Contact us today if your firm is best qualified to serve our clients.

Organizations

Through our nonprofit, Prison Professors Charitable Corporation, we develop a comprehensive ecosystem to improve outcomes for all justice-impacted people. Visit our affiliated website at PrisonProfessorsTalent.com to learn of our ecosystem and steps to advocate for earning freedom through merit, work-release, and home-confinement programs.

Advocacy Groups

Our nation incarcerates too many people, and those people serve sentences that are far too long. We have a long history of advocating for reforms that would allow people to work toward earning freedom through merit. Our book, Earning Freedom, relates to The First Step Act, and we're doing more to expand those initiatives.

Justin Paperny
Co-Founder

My name is Justin Paperny. I'm pleased to share how our team assists defense attorneys and people going through various stages of the criminal justice system. We know that defense attorneys fight valiantly to work toward the best possible outcomes for their clients.

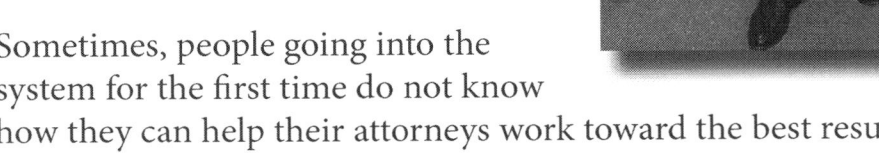

Sometimes, people going into the system for the first time do not know how they can help their attorneys work toward the best results.

Ask me how I know!

After graduating from USC, I began my career as a stockbroker. Unfortunately, I made some bad choices that led me into a government investigation. Living in denial, I made a series of catastrophic decisions that dug me into a deeper hole. Rather than helping my defense attorney, I made his job harder, which exposed me to a harsher sentence.

I wish I knew then what I know now. A federal judge sentenced me to serve an 18-month sentence for securities fraud.

While incarcerated, I met Michael Santos, who became my friend, mentor, and business partner. Although I was new to the system, he had been incarcerated for longer than 20 years. During his imprisonment, he earned academic degrees, published numerous books, and had a solid plan to succeed upon release.

www.WhiteCollarAdvice.com / Support@WhiteCollarAdvice.com / 818-424-2220

We agreed to launch a business that would help others prepare for the journey ahead. We wanted to provide them with resources and services they could use to get outstanding results at various stages of the journey.

Since then, we've built an entire ecosystem that includes various entities--all with one mission in mind: helping more people work toward the best possible outcome, regardless of what stage of the journey they're in, and regardless of budget.

This brochure will feature our talented team and the various entities we created to assist people who want to help their attorneys, and help themselves.

The strategies our team uses worked for me, and I'm confident that anyone can use them to work toward a better outcome.

Sincerely,

Justin Paperny

Pre Sentence Investigation to Alec Burlakoff

Alec Burlakoff

Alec's Story:
I once led a $3 billion sales organization. In 2018, our company, Insys Pharmaceutical, was the fastest growing company on the NASDAQ. Then, a government investigation began and it sucked me in.

Authorities threatened me with decades in prison. I made many bad decisions that could have exacerbated my troubles. I was in denial, not knowing what to do.

Then I found videos on White Collar Advice. I started to binge watch, learning from Justin as he spoke about the methodical strategies a person could use to get the best possible outcome.

Instead of decades in prison, my judge sentenced me to serve 26 months.

Why?

The mitigation strategy we engineered made a favorable impression on my judge. The Bureau of Prisons released me after 10 months.

The experience taught me a great deal about crisis management. It's the reason I joined the company.

If you've got questions about the journey ahead, we can help.

- Alec Burlakoff (Director of Sales)

www.WhiteCollarAdvice.com / Support@WhiteCollarAdvice.com / 818-424-2220

PSR Preparation

In the federal judicial system, everything changes if a person pleads guilty, or a jury convicts a person of committing a crime. At that moment, the presumption of innocence evaporates. Labels change for the person. For many, it will feel as if the common humanity is gone because authority figures will use terms such as defendant, convicted criminal, or inmate.

A federal probation officer will gather information from the investigating officers and from the prosecutor. Then, the officer will provide the individual with preliminary forms and schedule time for an interview. The interview may take place in person, or it may take place over a telephone call. The defense attorney may or may not be present for the interview.

Following the interview, the probation officer may gather additional information by contacting others, including victims of the crime, family members, employers, or others.

The investigation will conclude with a report commonly known as the PSR. The judge will consider the PSR when deliberating on the appropriate sentence. Yet the PSR will have much more significance that could influence the person's release date through administrative (rather than judicial means).

An individual should consider the PSR early, and sow seeds that will influence the judge, the Bureau of Prisons, and the probation officer on the other side of the journey.

Helpful links:
» Watch a clip of a US District Court Judge responding to our questions about PSR preparation and influence.

www.WhiteCollarAdvice.com / Support@WhiteCollarAdvice.com / 818-424-2220

RDAP

The Federal Bureau of Prisons offers a program that, potentially, can advance a person's release date. It's a merit-based program, but not all people qualify. Sadly, some people disqualified themselves because they didn't understand the program.

They set themselves up for failure rather than success.

I'm referring to a program known as the Residential Drug Abuse Program (RDAP).

We encourage people to learn everything they can possibly learn about the program. That way, if they want to take steps to make sure they qualify, they know what to do–before it's too late.

Remember our motto: It's never too early, and it's never too late to begin working toward a better outcome.

Take the case of Scott Carper.

As a former business professional, Scott did not know anything about the criminal justice system when authorities brought him into the legal system. Thanks to his early preparations, he succeeded in completing RDAP. Those early preparations influenced his ability to qualify for the program, and his ability to get home much earlier than would have otherwise been the case.

We encourage you to listen to Scott's story in his own words.

www.WhiteCollarAdvice.com / Support@WhiteCollarAdvice.com / 818-424-2220

Digital Courses

The criminal justice system is complicated. Building a case for leniency, or mercy, requires a comprehensive mitigation strategy. Our digital courses can help. Access lessons, watch videos, and learn from subject-matter experts, including federal judges, wardens, probation officers, and people who've gone through every stage of the journey.

Always strive to help your defense attorney by creating resources to support arguments for leniency.

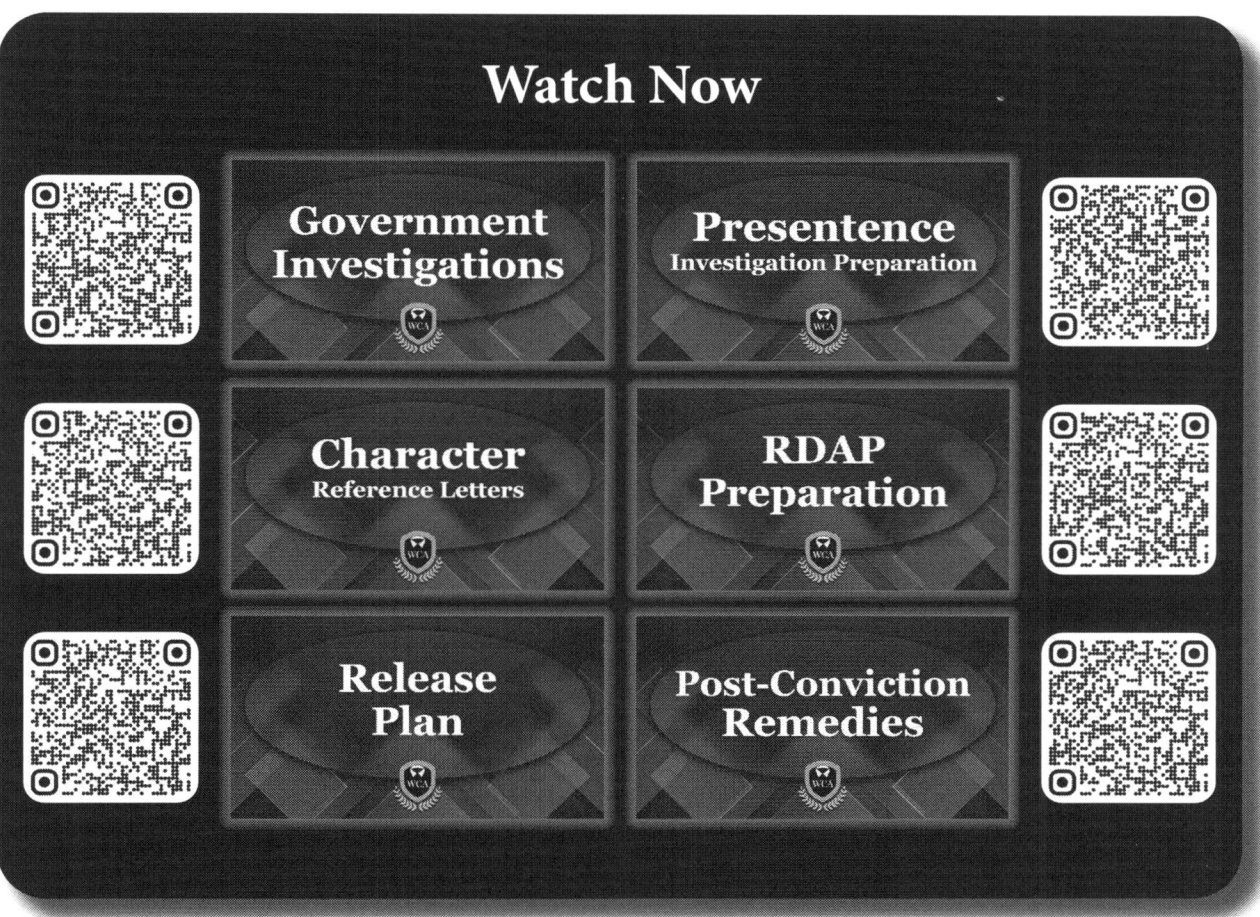

Sentencing Preparation Example

Mark Alan Blander
51 Cliff Hill Drive
Newport Beach, CA 92663

May 5, 2023

Name of Judge
United States District Court
Central District of California
411 West Fourth Street
Santa Ana, CA 92701

Regarding: United States of America—v—Mark Blander
Case Number:

Dear Judge (insert name):

My name is Mark Blander and I write because I'm tormented with shame and grief. I'm deeply remorseful for the crimes that I committed. Introspection leaves me no choice but to acknowledge that I've been a man of poor character, a man who failed to live up to his fullest potential. My actions have victimized others and I'm sorry. I'll spend the rest of my life working to atone or to reconcile with society—to the best of my ability.

Prior to pleading guilty, I failed to appreciate the severity of my crimes. Yet over the past two years, while waiting for my judicial proceedings to unfold, I've not had a single day without suffering from a guilty conscience. Rest isn't possible without my being heavily medicated. Even though I take medication for anxiety and other disorders, I don't know how to stop the mental anguish that comes from accepting the colossal disappointment I've been and the bad decisions that I've made throughout my life.

Influencing Sentencing

Through our advocacy work, we've interviewed scores of federal judges. Two of those federal judges agreed to participate in video interviews with us. We asked them whether a person could do or say anything that might influence the judge's sentencing decision.

If a person faces a criminal charge and has not yet been sentenced, we highly recommend these videos we recorded with US District Court Judge Bennett, and US District Court Judge Stephen Bough. Get help preparing for the best outcomes.

Click QR Code to watch full interview with Judge Bennett. Listen and learn from what he advises people to do before sentencing in his court.

Click QR Code to watch the full interview with Judge Stephen Bough. Listen and learn from what he advises people to do before sentencing in his court.

Without exception, the judges with whom we've spoken told us that they wanted to know more about the people who stand before them at sentencing. They want to hear what the defendant has to say about:

- » Victims of the crime,
- » What influences led to the crime,
- » What the person has learned from the experience,
- » What has the person done to make amends,
- » How can the judge be sure that he will go on to live a law-abiding life?

www.WhiteCollarAdvice.com / Support@WhiteCollarAdvice.com / 818-424-2220

Personal Advocacy Campaigns

Character Reference Letters

By writing a first-person story that reveals more about your empathy with the victims, what you've learned from this experience, and steps you're taking to make amends, you will go a long way toward helping your attorney advocate for leniency. But your judge will also want to hear from people who know you best. Launch an effective campaign to generate meaningful character-reference letters. They should avoid opinions about what sentence length would be appropriate, and focus on what the writer knows about your character.

Our team can help!

Community Service

Investigators and prosecutors will invest hundreds of hours to build a case against you. They want the judge to consider the crime, and nothing more.

If you're serious about mitigation, build a story to show all the ways that you've worked to make amends and reconcile with society. Your lawyer will want to advocate for the lowest possible sentence. Your job is to provide your lawyer with resources that will advance you as a candidate for leniency.

Mitigation Strategies

When authorities bring criminal charges, in theory, they're representing all citizens. They believe in the social contract, which requires every citizen to abide by the law. When due process shows that a person broke the law, every law-abiding citizen suffers.

What mitigation strategies have you engineered to overcome this hurdle?

Your defense attorney will argue that you're deserving of a lower sentence. Yet you have a duty to provide your defense team with resources that show the creative ways that you've been working to make amends, or to reconcile with society.

You may not be able to change the past, but if you're creative, you will develop mitigation strategies that make you a better candidate for mercy.

The only limit to developing a comprehensive mitigation strategy is your level of commitment. We would not ask you to do anything that did not work for members of our team. Review our various websites for ideas on how you begin building resources that will help you build a stronger case for leniency at sentencing, and perhaps through administrative proceedings that follow after sentencing.

Release Preparations

Name
Registration Number 64877-037
Prison Location
Release Plan

July 24, 2023

Dear Unit Team:

Before surrendering, I researched the best practice for serving time in federal prison. From that research, I found different websites to help me prepare. As I studied the information, I learned about the role of the Unit Team in the Bureau of Prisons and the importance of developing a comprehensive release plan.

I created this plan to guide me through the journey, and to prepare for a successful outcome from every aspect of this system, including imprisonment, home confinement, and supervised release.

I pleaded guilty, and I accept responsibility for my mistakes. I am ashamed of my actions that brought me here, but I know that remorse alone cannot make amends for my crime. With my Unit Team's guidance and the accountability of my loved ones, I will remain committed to making this time productive, reconciling with society, and strengthening relationships with my family.

I developed my release plan as an accountability tool that describes my self-directed pathway to prepare for the best outcomes after my release. I will continue updating and expanding the document as I meet milestones on my journey and set new goals consistent with my commitments.

The plan includes the following information:

1. Identifying Information
2. Images
3. Projected Release Planning
4. Background
5. My Crime
6. Making Amends
7. Community Support
8. Medical Prescriptions
9. Financial Obligations
10. Risk and Needs Assessment
11. Personal Plan
12. Advisors

I hope the Unit Team finds this plan helpful in guiding me back to my family and community as soon as possible.

PrisonProfessorsTalent.com

Prison Professors Talent

A comprehensive mitigation strategy should include a plan for every stage of the journey, including after the sentencing hearing. Too many people go into the system without a clear idea or plan for what will happen after the judge imposes sentences.

Those who want to work toward the highest level of liberty at the soonest possible time will develop resources to help them self-advocate after sentencing. Working toward a better outcome requires a person to develop an extraordinary and compelling adjustment strategy. This strategy should memorialize all the efforts a person has made to atone.

Our nonprofit supports Prison Professors Talent, a website that our clients can use to show the reasons why they're worthy of consideration for higher levels of liberty. We offer courses and prompts to assist a person, and our team provides the administrative support necessary for effective self-advocacy.

Visit PrisonProfessorsTalent.com to see examples of how members of our community use this resource to advance campaigns for liberty at various stages of the journey.

Timelines

We create timelines to help stakeholders understand the pathway to redemption.

Step 1:
We assist clients who want to engineer a mitigation strategy.

Step 2:
We create timelines to memorialize the efforts a person has taken to reconcile with society.

Step 3:
We create graphics that defense attorneys can use to illustrate reasons why a person is an extraordinary candidate for leniency and mercy.

Accepted Responsibility

www.WhiteCollarAdvice.com / Support@WhiteCollarAdvice.com / 818-424-2220

Legal document:
In 2018 I learned that authorities were investigating my role in a white-collar crime.

Prosecutors:
I cooperated fully with investigators and prosecutors, explaining how I became involved in this crime.

PSR document:
I openly expressed my story to the probation officer, explaining what I learned from this experience and what I'm doing to make things right.

Story:
I wrote an extensive first-person narrative, expressing remorse and explaining how I identify with the pain I caused to victims because of my criminal negligence.

Community Service:
I began volunteering with the Prison Professors nonprofit to work toward reconciling with society, working to create pathways for people to work toward success upon release.

Blueprints:
I created a release plan to show the pathway that I'm on to emerge from this experience as a law-abiding, contributing citizen.

www.WhiteCollarAdvice.com / Support@WhiteCollarAdvice.com / 818-424-2220

Be Extraordinary

Planning is essential for any person who wants to prepare for success after prison. Unfortunately, people in prison do not get that message as often as they should. They need examples to show how early planning contributes to success upon release. Our courses show how people in prison can work to:

- » Define the best possible outcome,
- » Create a plan that will advance them from struggle to increasing levels of liberty,
- » Identify priorities so they know how incremental progress leads to new opportunities,
- » Build tools, tactics, and resources that open more opportunities,
- » Measure progress with personal accountability metrics,
- » Execute their plans daily, making adjustments as necessary.

Our courses prompt people in jails and prisons with lessons and exercises they can use to memorialize their progress, helping them to build effective release plans. Through personal-development, they recalibrate and prepare to emerge as law-abiding, contributing citizens. We're proud to collaborate with leaders of federal and state prisons to help more people prepare for success upon release.

We strive to help people in custody understand the importance of sowing seeds for success. No one should work harder than the individual to prepare for a life of meaning, relevance, and contribution.

We learned these lessons from studying leadership.

Media Contributions

When members of the media need a credible commentator, they find that we offer both depth and breadth of experience. We are based in Southern California, and easily accessible for in-person interviews, or through video calls.

Media groups that feature our work:

www.WhiteCollarAdvice.com / Support@WhiteCollarAdvice.com / 818-424-2220

Academic / Professional

We're proud to work directly with the Bureau of prisons as an approved First-Step Act program, as shown on the Bureau of Prisons' website. Our course, Preparing for Success after Prison is available in all federal prisons. Successful participants earn time off their sentence by completing the program.

Our team frequently works with universities, business organizations, and law enforcement to provide in-person training or to lead seminars. We specialize in helping others understand various aspects of the criminal justice system, and in helping audiences understand the merits of reform that would include work-release programs, community service, and more mechanisms that allow people to earn freedom through merit.

Some of the groups with whom we've worked:

www.WhiteCollarAdvice.com / Support@WhiteCollarAdvice.com / 818-424-2220

Our Team

Brad Rouse earned his undergraduate degree from Harvard. An expert communicator and performing artist, he won the Louis Sudler Prize. As an award-winning theater artist, Brad developed exceptional writing skills and personal knowledge of government investigations.

Forrest Behne, a Washington & Lee University graduate, overcame involvement in the criminal justice system through executive clemency. He now advances public health research and supports White Collar Advice clients as a writer and administrator.

Joseph DeGregorio, a former Wall Street banker turned advocate, significantly reduced his federal sentence through self-improvement and strategic efforts. He now aids others affected by the justice system, offering guidance and mentorship.

UCSB graduate and UCLA-certified in Real Estate Law, Scott Carper founded SCMN Consulting after a notable tenure at CBS Outdoor. Post-conviction, he authored educational pieces and earned a paralegal certificate in prison, now advocating for positive personal transformation.

Tulio Cardozo transformed his life during a lengthy prison term by mastering computer programming. Now a skilled IT professional, he effectively applies his self-taught expertise to our team, specializing in designing innovative CRM systems.

Patty Westmoreland, with degrees from Kennesaw State and UNC-Chapel Hill, brings 15 years of banking experience to White Collar Advice, where she provides resources and support to individuals navigating the criminal justice system.

www.WhiteCollarAdvice.com / Support@WhiteCollarAdvice.com / 818-424-2220

Non Profit

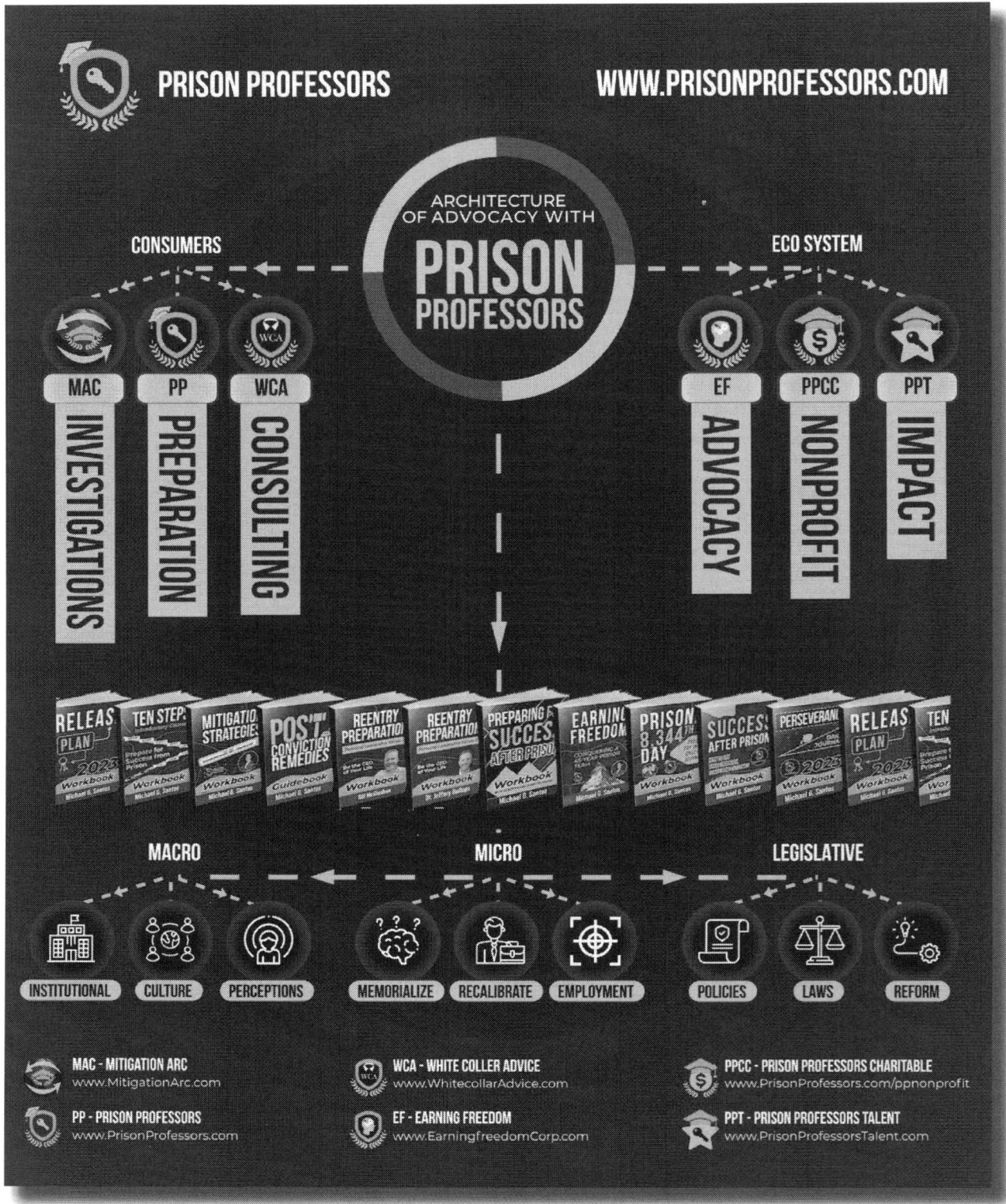

Non Profit Advocacy

Culture
Self-directed, goal-oriented adjustment strategies

Planning
Memorializing commitments to prepare for success

Employment
Collaborations to qualify people for good jobs upon release

At Prison Professors Charitable Corporation, we envision a world where justice and rehabilitation go hand in hand. We empower those touched by the criminal justice system — from individuals bracing for incarceration to those navigating reentry into society, along with their families. We ignite hope and open doors to new possibilities through innovative educational content and training programs.

Our partnerships with federal and state prison systems allow us to have a direct impact on the lives of more than 1 million people annually. We are a movement, dedicated to reimagining America's prison system and helping people prepare for employment and success upon release. By championing excellence and advocating for increasing levels of liberty through merit, we are committed to advocacy that will reduce our nation's prison population and lower recidivism rates.

We began as a public benefits corporation to help all justice-impacted people.

We create educational content and training programs to help people prepare for law-abiding, contributing lives. We strive to stop intergenerational cycles of recidivism by showing people how they can recalibrate while incarcerated.

Further, we advocate to create programs that will incentivize excellence, and encourage people to work toward earning freedom through merit.

Our programs currently reach more than 300,000 people in jails and prisons across the United States. We collaborate with:

- » The Federal Bureau of Prisons,
- » The California Department of Corrections, with
- » The Edovo Foundation, and with others.

The more people we reach, the more requests we receive from indigent people who want access to the books and courses we create.

Our various entities have been the largest financial sponsors for our nonprofit. We invite others who want to improve the outcomes of America's criminal justice system to join us. All contributions support our advocacy in accordance with our nonprofit's by-laws.

We consider our nation's commitment to mass incarceration as one of the great social injustices of our time, and we strive to improve outcomes.

Legal Directory

Hire the Top 1% White Collar Attorneys

Work with the best White Collar Attorneys who have been handpicked to deliver the highest form of justice for you.

Our various social media platforms have generated millions of views from people who do not know how to navigate the complexities of a criminal investigation or charge. They reach out to us for guidance, including how to hire a defense attorney.

For that reason, we launched our legal directory: "www.TOPWCA.com"

TOPWCA stands for top white collar attorney. We're striving to feature no more than five defense attorneys in each of the 94 different federal judicial districts.

If you would like us to include you in our legal directory so that members of our community can learn about your expertise, If you would like us to feature your practice in our legal directory, please schedule a call by opening the QR code above, or sending a text.

Justin Paperny: 818-424-2220 / JP@WhiteCollarAdvice.com

Made in the USA
Columbia, SC
03 June 2024

36579500R00020